national TESTS practice papers

FOR THE YEAR 2002

Maths, English and Science

Book 1 Levels 3–5

AGE 10-11
Key Stage 2

practice Papers

Contents	Page
Introduction	
The National Tests: A Summary	ii
Maths Test	
Maths at Key Stage 2	1
Test A (without calculator)	2
Test B (with calculator)	11
Mental Maths Test	20
Answers	22
National Curriculum Levels	26
English Test	
Reading Test	27
Writing Test	43
Spelling Test	47
Handwriting Test	49
Answers	50
National Curriculum Levels	53
Science Test	
Science at Key Stage 2	54
Science Test	55
Answers	63
National Curriculum Levels	63

Introduction

The National Tests: A Summary

What are the National Tests?
Children who attend state schools in England and Wales sit National Tests (also known as SATs) at the ages of 7, 11 and 14, usually at the beginning of May. They may also sit optional tests in the intervening years – many schools have chosen to adopt these tests. The test results are accompanied by an assessment by the child's teacher.

The results are used by the school to assess each child's level of knowledge and progress in English and Maths at Key Stage 1 and English, Maths and Science at Key Stages 2 and 3. They also provide useful guidance for the child's next teacher.

The educational calendar for children aged 5–14 is structured as follows:

Key Stage	Year	Age by end of year	National Test
1 (KS1)	1	6	
	2	7	KEY STAGE 1
2 (KS2)	3	8	Optional Year 3
	4	9	Optional Year 4
	5	10	Optional Year 5
	6	11	KEY STAGE 2
3 (KS3)	7	12	
	8	13	
	9	14	KEY STAGE 3

Test Timetable
Key Stage 2 tests take place in one week in May. All children sit the same test at the same time. In 2002, the tests will take place in the week of **13–17 May**. Your child's school will be able to provide you with a detailed timetable.

Levels
National average levels have been set for children's results in the National Tests. The levels are as follows:

LEVEL	AGE 7 (Key Stage 1)	AGE 11 (Key Stage 2)	AGE 14 (Key Stage 3)
8			
7			
6			
5			
4			
3			
2			
2a			
2b			
2c			
1			

- BELOW EXPECTED LEVEL
- EXPECTED LEVEL
- ABOVE EXPECTED LEVEL
- EXCEPTIONAL

Results
Your child's school will send you a report indicating his or her levels in the tests and the teacher assessment.

The school's overall test results will be included in local and national league tables, which are published in most newspapers.

What can parents do to help?
While it is never a good idea to encourage cramming, you can help your child to succeed by:

- Making sure he or she has enough food, sleep and leisure time during the test period.
- Practising important skills such as writing and reading stories, spelling and mental arithmetic.
- Telling him or her what to expect in the test, such as important symbols and key words.
- Helping him or her to be comfortable in test conditions including working within a time limit, reading questions carefully and understanding different ways of answering.

Maths Test

Maths at Key Stage 2

The Key Stage 2 National Tests cover Number, Measures, Shape and Space and Data Handling. Most children will take two one-hour written tests and a short, orally delivered mental test. Test A is a written non-calculator paper and Test B is a written paper where children can use a calculator, should they wish. There is also a written extension test, Test C, that some more able children might be given.

Levels

Children taking the Maths Tests A and B and the Mental Maths Test can achieve below level 3, level 3, level 4 or level 5, with a typical 11-year-old attaining level 4. For children attaining a very high score, a further test (Test C) can be given to ascertain whether he or she is performing at level 6.

To gain an idea of the level at which your child is working, use the table on page 26, which shows you how to convert your child's marks into a National Curriculum level.

Setting the Tests

Written Test

Allow one hour for each test. Do not expect your child to take them one after another. In the National Test week, children will take the mathematics tests over two or three days. Your child will need a ruler, pencil, rubber, protractor and, if possible, a small mirror or piece of tracing paper, together with a calculator (for Test B).

Encourage your child to work systematically through each test, returning later to questions which cause difficulty.

If your child has difficulty in reading the questions, you can read them aloud, provided the mathematical words are not altered or explained. Where necessary, your child can dictate their answers and these can be written down for him or her. For large numbers, however, your child should be clear which digits are intended to be written, e.g. for a number such as three thousand and six your child should indicate that this is written as three, zero, zero, six.

Mental Maths Test

The mental test should take approximately 10–15 minutes to give, by reading aloud the questions on page 20, which you should copy for ease of use. Your child will only need a pencil and rubber for the mental test.

Allow only the time suggested for each question, reading each one twice.

Marking the tests

Next to each question in the written tests is a number indicating how many marks the question or part of the question is worth. Enter your child's mark into the circle above, using the answer pages to help you decide how many points to award.

Find your child's total score from the written tests and mental test and refer to page 26 for information about the level your child might be working at.

Maths Test
Test A (without calculator)

1 Fill in the missing numbers.

18 ÷ [6] = 3

12 + 15 = 38 − [11]

(2 × 20) − 10 = 10 + [20]

2 Write two more numbers into this diagram so that the numbers in each row and column add up to 100.

10 60 30
50 [20] [30]
40 20 40

3 Continue this sequence.

3 4 6 9 [13] [18]

Explain how you worked out the missing numbers.

goes up in a number sequence

Maths Test A

4 At a netball tournament there are 7 players in each team.

112 players take part in the tournament.

How many teams take part in the tournament?

112 ÷ 7 =
70 people   10 teams

16

2

5 Lucy is playing darts. She throws three darts and hits **three different** numbers. She notices that the **mean** of the numbers is **9.**

What **different** numbers could Lucy have hit?

16   **4**   **7**

1

TOTAL

3

3

Maths Test A

6 A shop sells ice cream.

This table shows the most popular types of ice cream sold in the shop during one week.

Flavour	Large cone	Small cone
Chocolate	15	14
Vanilla	19	12
Strawberry	11	8

How many **large** cones were sold during the week? **45**

Which flavour was the most popular during the week? **Vanilla**

7 One side of a shape has been drawn below. The shape has **three right angles** and **more than four** sides. Using a ruler, draw the other sides to complete the shape.

TOTAL 4

Maths Test A

8 Mr Thomas bought three shirts.

One shirt cost £4.25. The second shirt cost twice as much.
How much did the second shirt cost? £ 8.50

Mr Thomas spent exactly £20 on all three shirts. 12.75
How much did the third shirt cost? £ 7.25

9 Fill in the missing number so that the numbers along each side add to make 19.5.

```
        4.5
     □      9.25
  9.75   4   5.75
```

1

1

2

TOTAL

4

Maths Test A

10 Playing cards come in different suits.

diamonds   clubs   spades   hearts

Here are five playing cards.

These cards are shuffled and spread out face down on a table. **One card** is picked from the set.

What is the probability that it is a **heart**?
Give your answer as a fraction.

What is the probability that it is a **diamond**?
Show your answer by drawing a cross on this line.

0   1

11 The hundreds digits are missing from two numbers in this number sentence. Write what they could be.

☐ 5 9 + ☐ 7 4 = 833

Maths Test A

12 Look at this multiplication fact.

$$26 \times 123 = 3198$$

Use this fact to find the answers to these questions:

$25 \times 123 = \boxed{}$

$26 \times 124 = \boxed{}$

$260 \times 123 = \boxed{}$

$2.6 \times 12.3 = \boxed{}$

13 Circle **two** fractions below that are equivalent.

$\dfrac{2}{5}$ $\dfrac{3}{8}$ $\dfrac{6}{10}$ $\dfrac{6}{16}$

$\dfrac{6}{12}$ $\dfrac{1}{10}$ $\dfrac{6}{8}$

14 Calculate **952 − 436** $\boxed{}$

TOTAL 6

Maths Test A

15 Using a ruler, mirror or tracing paper, **draw and shade** the reflection of the shape below in the mirror line.

mirror line

What area of the grid is now shaded? ☐ cm²

What fraction of the grid is now shaded? ☐

How many degrees is **angle a**?
You may use an angle measurer (protractor). ☐

16 Here are two squares drawn on a graph.
Fill in the missing **co-ordinates** of **point C**.

A (12, 10)

B (3, 4)   C (,)

17 In a gymnastics competition, the gymnasts are awarded points for **difficulty**, **style** and **technical merit.** These points are added together to find a total score.

Here are the numbers of points awarded to three children.

Name	Difficulty	Style	Technical Merit
Alice	3.8	5.1	4.7
Ajay	4.3	4.9	5.2
Emily	5.4	4.6	4.8

What is the **total** number of points awarded to Emily?

For **difficulty**, who was awarded **closest** to 4 points?

What was the difference between Emily's and Alice's **total** scores?

Maths Test A

18 Mrs Wood is buying some fruit.

The fruit comes in bags of different sizes. This table shows the prices of the different bags.

	Bananas	Apples
500 g	69p	35p
750 g	99p	50p
1 kg	£1.25	65p

Mrs Wood buys **three bags** of fruit
– **one** 500 g bag, **one** 750 g bag and **one** 1 kg bag.

What is the total **mass** of fruit she buys?

She spends a total of **£2.33**.
Which **three** bags does she buy?

Maths Test
Test B (with calculator)

1 Write three numbers to make the number sentence correct.

☐ + ☐ + ☐ = 104

2 An arrow is pointing to each of the number lines below.
Write the numbers indicated by the arrows into the boxes.

0 — 100 — ☐↓ — 200

650 — ☐↓ — 750

2000 — ☐↓ — 3000

3 Here are some number riddles.
Write the number for each riddle in the box.

The number is less than 40.
It is a multiple of 6.
It is a multiple of 4.
It is a multiple of 9.

☐

The number is between 30 and 50.
It is a square number.
It is an odd number.

☐

Maths Test B

4 Write what the **missing numbers** could be to make the number sentences correct.

☐ − ☐ + ☐ = 25

☐ ÷ ☐ = 8

5 x 3 + ☐ = 6 x ☐

5 **3781** people go to a football match.
They each pay **£3.50** to get in.

What is the total amount of money paid?

£ ☐

Programmes cost 75p each.
A **total** of **£604.50** is raised from selling programmes.

How many programmes are sold?

Maths Test B

6 This diagram shows the **number of kilometres** between some cities in the United Kingdom.

	Aberdeen	Bristol	Glasgow	Manchester	Dover
Aberdeen	—	490	150	332	574
Bristol	490	—	366	167	195
Glasgow	150	366	—	210	467
Manchester	332	167	210	—	265
Dover	574	195	467	265	—

Explain why each number appears twice in the table.

_____

_____

A delivery driver visits three cities on the same journey. She starts at **Bristol**, drives to **Manchester** and then on to **Dover**. How far does she travel?

☐ km

7 Use all of these digits to make the four-digit number closest to 5000.

8 4 3 5

Maths Test B

8 Here is an arrangement of dots. Join some of these dots with straight lines to draw a **regular hexagon.** Use a ruler.

9 Hannah is colouring a flag.

The pattern she is colouring has **rotational symmetry**.

She still has **one square** to colour.

Shade **one** square so that the pattern will have **rotational symmetry.**

10 This number sequence is made by counting on in steps of **equal size.** Fill in the **missing numbers.**

| 4 | | | 22 | |

Maths Test B

11 David is playing a game using a set of ten **different** number cards showing **1 to 10**. He turns over two cards and adds the numbers to find the **total**.

These are his first four goes:

Card 1	Card 2	Total
6	7	13
3	5	8
4	9	13
7	2	9

What is the **lowest total** David can get? ☐

Jenny says,
"You are equally likely to get a total of 10 as a total of 3."
Is she correct?

| yes | no |

Explain your answer.

_____

_____

12 Fill in the missing numbers to make these statements correct.

53912 ÷ ☐ = 586

5748 × ☐ = 120708

1

1

1

1
TOTAL

4

15

Maths Test B

13 Look carefully at the shapes below.

Square

Trapezium **B**

A

Regular octagon

C

D

Isosceles triangle

Write the letter of shapes **B**, **C** and **D** into the correct section of the table below. One has been done for you.

	No pairs of parallel sides	One pair of parallel sides	More than one pair of parallel sides
3 sides			
4 sides			A
More than 4 sides			

14 Calculate 32% of 950.

15 Mr Hall is making some blackcurrant drink.

He uses **125 ml** of blackcurrant squash and then fills the jug to the top with water.

Use a ruler to draw a **line** to show where the **125 ml** of blackcurrant squash would come to on the **litre** container.

How many times more water than blackcurrant squash does Mr Hall use?

Mr Hall drinks **one quarter** of the litre of blackcurrant drink. How much drink does he have now?

Give your answer in **litres.**

☐ l

Maths Test B

16 Carol is arranging exactly **four** number cards to make different fractions **less than one**. These are the numbers.

10 2 5 4

Using **each** number card only **once**, show where each would go to make this statement correct.

☐/☐ is the same value as ☐/☐

Find another way to place these cards to make **different** fractions that have the same value.

☐/☐ is the same value as ☐/☐

17 Here is part of a flower bed.

The flower bed has **16 rows** of daffodils. Each row has **17** daffodils in it. How many daffodils are there in **13** flower beds?

18 Jack and Chloe go to a car boot sale. They buy some books.

Entrance fee 75p and 20p for each book

Jack pays the **entrance fee** and buys **twelve books**.

How much does he spend?

Chloe pays the **entrance fee** and buys some books.

She spends exactly **£2.55**.

How many books does she buy?

Entrance fee 75p and 20p for each book

Write a formula to show the total cost (**C**) in pence of visiting the car boot sale if you buy *n* books.

C =

Mental Maths Test
Questions

"For this first set of questions you have five seconds to work out each answer and write it down."

1 Write the number four thousand and nine in figures.

2 What is eighteen more than thirty?

3 What is twice one point seven?

4 Seven tenths of the children in a class are boys. What percentage are boys?

5 How many sides do three octagons have in total?

6 What is half of seventy two?

"For the next set of questions you have ten seconds to work out each answer and write it down."

7 What is double one hundred and eighty?

8 How many minutes are there in two and a half hours?

9 Add five and nineteen and then divide by three.

10 A snail crawls eighty one centimetres. How much further does it have to crawl to reach one metre?

11 One third of a number is seven. What is the number?

12 On the answer sheet is part of a scale. What number is the arrow pointing to?

13 A shop has a sale. All items are twenty five per cent of their original price. A video costs four pounds in the sale. What was its original price?

14 Sam cycles six miles every day. How far does he cycle in a week?

15 Look at the answer sheet. Draw a ring around the approximate height of a door.

"For the next set of questions you have fifteen seconds to work out each answer and write it down."

16 Look at the answer sheet. Draw a ring around the number that is nearest to seven.

17 Thirty per cent of a number is fifteen. What is the number?

18 Which year is seventeen years before the year two thousand and two?

19 Look at the answer sheet. What is the size of angle A?

20 Look at the answer sheet. Draw a ring around three numbers that are multiples of twenty.

Mental Maths Test
Answer Sheet

5-second questions

1. ☐
2. ☐
3. ☐
4. ☐
5. ☐
6. ☐

10-second questions

7. ☐
8. ☐ minutes
9. ☐
10. ☐ centimetres
11. ☐
12. ☐ (scale: 4.6 to 4.7 with arrow)
13. £ ☐
14. ☐ miles
15. 2000 cm   20 m   200 cm   20 cm   2 cm

15-second questions

16. 0.7   7.9   6.6   7.5   7.74
17. ☐
18. ☐
19. A= ☐ (triangle with 90°, 50°, A)
20. 240   130   290   88   580   200

TOTAL / 20

21

Answers
Maths Test

Question number	Answer	Mark	Parent's notes and additional information
Test A			
1a	6	1	
1b	11	1	
1c	20	1	(2 x 20) – 10 = 30, so 10 + ☐ = 30
2	20, 30	1	
3a	13, 18	1	
3b	A mark for either: an explanation that the differences between numbers in the sequence go up in ones or a reference to counting on, e.g. 'no numbers missed out, one number missed out, two numbers missed out etc.'	1	Children's answers to questions like these should include <u>numbers</u> to support their explanations. Just writing 'I saw a pattern. The numbers go up' is generally not enough to score a mark.
4	16 Award 1 mark if your child has attempted to divide 112 by 7.	2	It does not matter whether this calculation is done mentally or using a written method.
5	Any three <u>different</u> numbers that have a total of 27, e.g. 8, 9, 10 or 20, 3, 4.	1	The mean (average) of a set of numbers is found by finding the total and dividing this by the number of numbers in the set. In this case there are 3 numbers so: The mean… 9 = **27** ÷3
6a	45	1	Children are required to interpret the table and then find the total of 15, 19 and 11.
6b	Vanilla	1	Children should check the totals of each row to find the most popular flavour.
7	Any shape with more than 4 sides and with exactly 3 right angles. 1 mark should be awarded if the shape has more than 4 sides and some right angles.	2	Examples of shapes: External right angles (those outside the shape) do not count
8a	£8.50 Note that amounts of money should never be written with both the **£** sign and a **p** sign, e.g. £8.50p is incorrect and would not earn a mark.	1	Children must double £4.25. Children of this age should try to learn doubles of all numbers to 100 and their corresponding halves, e.g. double 25 = 50 and half of 50 = 25. They can then use this knowledge for questions of this kind.
8b	£7.25	1	
9	5.25 Award 1 mark for workings that include the number 14.25.	2	
10a	$\frac{1}{5}$	1	There are 5 cards. The probability of picking the only heart is one out of five. Probabilities generally can be written in words or as fractions or decimals, e.g. **one out of five, $\frac{1}{5}$ or 0.20**.
10b		1	There are 5 cards. The probability of picking one of the two diamonds is two out of five.
11	Your child should have written two digits that add to make 7, e.g. **159 + 674** 259 + 574 359 + 474 459 + 374 559 + 274 or **659 + 174**	1	If your child has written two digits that add to make 8, encourage him or her to add the two numbers together, e.g. 459 + 474 Point out that the answer comes to 933.
12a	3075	1	Your child should notice that 25 × 123 is 123 less than 26 × 123. Ideally he or she should subtract 123 from 3198 to get 3075. A mark can be awarded if the answer was found using a different method.
12b	3224	1	Again, your child should notice that 26 × 124 is 26 more than 26 × 123. If he or she finds this difficult, discuss it in a context, e.g. 124 things costing £26, cost £26 more than 123 things costing £26.

Maths Test Answers

Question number	Answer	Mark	Parent's notes and additional information
12c	31980	1	This answer is ten times larger than the given multiplication fact.
12d	31.98	1	Encourage your child to work out an approximate answer to decide where the decimal point should go, e.g. 2.6×12.3 is approximately $3 \times 12 = 36$, so the answer is not 319.8 or 3.198, but 31.98.
13	$\frac{3}{8}$ and $\frac{6}{16}$ are equivalent.	1	Equivalent means that the fractions have the same value, e.g. if you have $\frac{3}{8}$ of a pizza it is the same value as $\frac{6}{16}$ of a pizza.
14	516	1	
15a		2	1 mark should be awarded if 5 or 6 out of the 7 corners of the shape are reflected correctly, e.g.
15b	16 cm^2	1	The area of a shape is the number of whole squares inside the shape. In this case it is centimetre squares or cm^2 that are counted. If your child gave the answer 22, he or she counted half squares as whole squares.
15c	$\frac{16}{40}$ or $\frac{4}{10}$ or $\frac{2}{5}$	1	There should be 16 out of 40 squares shaded.
15d	45° Accept answers that are 1 degree either side of 45°, e.g. 44° or 46°.	1	A protractor is not essential for this question. Show your child that the angle is half a right angle and that the exact answer is $90 \div 2 = 45°$.
16	(21, 4) Award 1 mark for each co-ordinate.	2	The second co-ordinate (how many up) is the same as B, i.e. 4. To work out the first co-ordinate (how far across) find the difference between 3 and 12 = 9 and then add this to 12 to get 21.
17a	14.8	1	5.4 + 4.6 + 4.8
17b	Alice Award a mark for writing 3.8.	1	Children may incorrectly answer 4.3. Show that 3.8 is 2 tenths from 4 whereas 4.3 is 3 tenths away from 4.
17c	1.2 Award one mark for workings that include an attempt to add Alice's scores and Emily's scores and to subtract one from the other.	2	5.4 + 4.6 + 4.8 = 14.8 3.8 + 5.1 + 4.7 = 13.6 1.2
18a	2250 g or 2.25 kg	1	500 g + 750 g + 1 kg (1000 g)
18b	500 g bananas (69p), 750 g bananas (99p), 1 kg apples (65p). Award 1 mark for attempts to add sets of three numbers, including prices and masses.	2	This question involves interpreting information and dealing with two criteria: the price (£2.33) and the different masses of the bags.
Test B			
1	Any three numbers that add to make 104.	1	
2a	140	1	Show your child that each 100 is split into 5 sections, so each must be worth 20.
2b	730	1	Show your child that each 100 is split into 10 sections, so each must be worth 10.
2c	2300	1	Show your child that each 1000 is split into 10 sections, so each must be worth 100.
3a	36	1	A multiple is a number that can be divided exactly into without a remainder, e.g. multiples of 6 include 6, 12, 18, 180, 486 etc.
3b	49	1	A square number is a number that is made from multiplying another number by itself, e.g. $4 = 2 \times 2$, $9 = 3 \times 3$, $25 = 5 \times 5$. Children should learn the square numbers to 100, i.e. 1, 4, 9, 16, 25, 36, 49, 64, 81, 100.

23

Maths Test Answers

Question number	Answer	Mark	Parent's notes and additional information
4a	Any three numbers that make 25, e.g. 50 − 30 + 5, 100 − 80 + 5.	1	
4b	Any numbers that divide to make 8, e.g. 8 ÷ 1, 16 ÷ 2, 24 ÷ 3, 80 ÷ 10.	1	
4c	Any numbers that make the statement correct, e.g. 5 × 3 + **3** = 6 × **3** 5 × 3 + **9** = 6 × **4** 5 × 3 + **15** = 6 × **5**.	1	Children often find this type of question difficult as they see the equals sign as an 'answer giver' rather than meaning 'is/has the same answer as'. Here 5 × 3 + ☐ 'has the same answer as' 6 × ☐.
5a	£13233.50 Do not award a mark for the answer £13233.5 or £13233.50p	1	Money answers must be written correctly for questions of this type. Calculator questions like these are often selected to see whether children can interpret the display in the context of money. Amounts of money should never be written with both the £ sign and a p sign.
5b	806 Award one mark if your child has shown that he or she is trying to divide in pounds or in pence, e.g. £604.50 ÷ £0.75 or 60450p ÷ 75p	2	Here children must change the amounts of money to be either in pounds or in pence. If your child has given the answer 8.06 by dividing £604.50 by 75 pounds, point out that the ticket price is given in pence and needs to be altered to £0.75.
6a	Any explanation showing that your child appreciates that the distances between the two towns, e.g. Bristol to Dover, will be the same distance in reverse, e.g. Dover to Bristol.	1	
6b	432 km Award one mark if the working shows 167 + 265 with an incorrect answer.	2	The most common mistake with questions of this type is to select the incorrect second distance. If your child answered 362 km, it is because he or she used the distances between Bristol and Manchester (167) and then between Bristol and Dover (195), rather than Bristol and Manchester (167) and on from Manchester to Dover (265).
7	4853	1	
8	A regular hexagon has 6 equal sides and 6 equal angles.	1	
9		1	Shapes or pattern that have rotational symmetry can look the same in more than one orientation when turned. Letters like S, H, X, O have rotational symmetry, but A, E, T, W do not. They cannot be turned to look the same in any other orientation.
10	10, 16, 28	1	To answer this question, your child should find the difference between 22 and 4 = 18. If the difference between boxes that are three apart is 18 then the difference between each box is 18 ÷ 3 = 6.
11a	3	1	David can pick a 1 and a 2 card, with a total of 3.
11b	no There must be an explanation with references to the fact that there are more ways to make 10 than there are to make 3, e.g. 3 can only be scored with a 1 and a 2 card, whereas 10 can be scored with a 1 and 9, 2 and 8, 3 and 7, 6 and 4 etc.	1	Children's answers to questions like these should include numbers, where possible. It is not enough to say that 'it is more likely to score 10 than 3'.
12a	92	1	Children often attempt questions of this type using trial and error, e.g. trying to divide 53912 by different numbers to get 586. This involves a great deal of time. Instead, encourage your child to see that division questions can be rearranged, e.g. 10 ÷ 5 = 2 and 10 ÷ 2 = 5. Here children should divide 53912 by 586 to get 92.
12b	21	1	Again, children attempt questions of this type using trial and error, e.g. trying to multiply 5748 by different numbers to get 120708. Instead, encourage your child to see that multiplication questions can be rearranged, e.g. 2 × 5 = 10 can be rearranged to make 10 ÷ 2 = 5. Here children should divide 120708 by 5748 to get 21.

Maths Test Answers

Question number	Answer	Mark	Parent's notes and additional information
13	(grid with C top-left, B middle, A middle-right, D bottom-right) Award one mark for each of the letters B, C and D correctly positioned.	3	Parallel lines are lines that if extended in either direction would never meet. Parallel lines are the same distance apart. A regular shape has equal sides and equal angles.
14	304	1	32% of 950 can be worked out in the following ways: $32 \div 100 \times 950$ or $32 \times 950 \div 100$ or 950×0.32
15a	(jug showing 125 ml)	1	Show children that the litre jug (1000 ml) is split into 10 sections, so each must be worth 100, so 125 will come a quarter of the way between 100 and 200.
15b	7 Award one mark if the working shows an attempt to subtract 125 ml from 1 litre and divide by 125 with an incorrect answer.	2	Marks are awarded for correct answers whatever the method.
15c	0.75 l	1	
16a	$\frac{4}{10}$ and $\frac{2}{5}$ or $\frac{2}{4}$ and $\frac{5}{10}$	1	The fractions can be in any order, e.g. $\frac{2}{5}$ and $\frac{4}{10}$ or $\frac{4}{10}$ and $\frac{2}{5}$
16b	$\frac{4}{10}$ and $\frac{2}{5}$ or $\frac{2}{4}$ and $\frac{5}{10}$ Do **not** award a mark if the answer has the same fractions as question 16a, even if given in a different order.	1	
17	3536 Award 1 mark for a method that shows $16 \times 17 \times 13$ with an incorrect answer.	2	
18a	£3.15 Do **not** award a mark for the answer £3.15p or £315.	1	Money answers must be written correctly for questions of this type. Calculator questions like these are often selected to see whether children can interpret the display in the context of money. Amounts of money should never be written with both the £ sign and a p sign.
18b	9 Award one mark for attempts to subtract 75 from 255 and divide this by 20.	2	Children may incorrectly answer 12.75 or 13. Remind them that the entrance fee (75p) should be subtracted first.
18c	Any of the following answers: $C = 75 + (20 \times n)$ $C = 75 + (n \times 20)$ $C = 75 + 20n$ $C = 20n + 75$ $C = 20 \times n + 75$ etc. Award one mark for $C = 20n$ or $C = 20 \times n$	2	Children find using letters in place of numbers quite difficult. Show them the following: For 1 book C (cost) $= 75 + (1 \times 20)$ For 2 books C (cost) $= 75 + (2 \times 20)$ For 3 books C (cost) $= 75 + (3 \times 20)$ etc. So for n books C (cost) $= 75 + (n \times 20)$ etc.

Mental Maths Test Answers

1. 4009
2. 48
3. 3.4
4. 70%
5. 24
6. 36
7. 360
8. 150
9. 8
10. 19 cm
11. 21
12. 4.67
13. £16
14. 42 miles
15. 200 cm
16. 6.6
17. 50
18. 1985
19. 40°
20. 240, 580, 200

One mark per correct answer.

National Curriculum Levels
Maths

Write your child's scores below

Mark scored in Test A [   ]   Total marks 40

Mark scored in Test B [   ]   Total marks 40

Mark scored in Mental test [   ]   Total marks 20

Total score [   ]   Total marks 100

The National Tests are levelled according to the child's total score.

Mark	24 or below	25–51	52–79	80–100
Level	Level 1/2	Level 3	Level 4	Level 5

For each test this can be broadly broken down as follows:

TEST A

Mark	0–10	11–20	21–31	32–40
Level	Level 1/2	Level 3	Level 4	Level 5

TEST B

Mark	0–10	11–20	21–31	32–40
Level	Level 1/2	Level 3	Level 4	Level 5

MENTAL TEST

Mark	0–4	5–10	11–15	16–20
Level	Level 1/2	Level 3	Level 4	Level 5

If your child needs more practice in any Maths topics, use the WHSmith Key Stage 2 Maths Revision Guide.

English Test
Reading Test

The Reading Test comprises a variety of texts – non-fiction, fiction and poetry – to test reading strategies across a range of genres. There will normally be a common theme.

The questions require four different kinds of answer:
- Short words or phrases (one mark for each correct response).
- Longer answers (one or two sentences) which require more understanding of the text (two marks).
- Detailed explanations of opinion (up to three marks).
- Multiple choice (one mark).

Although some questions will have a 'right answer', all children will express their responses in a different way.

Setting the test

Allow 15 minutes for reading the passages and 45 minutes for answering the questions.

1. Encourage your child to read each passage carefully.
2. Point out the different types of question: those which give a choice of answers to tick and those which need a written answer. Written answers need not be complete sentences. Some written answers are worth three or more marks if detail or examples are required.
3. Do not help your child to read the text, although you may help with the spelling of the answers.
4. Point out that your child may rub out or alter any mistakes.
5. Tell your child:
   - to find the answers in the text, rather than guessing;
   - to tick only one box in multiple choice questions;
   - to try to answer every question;
   - to leave any questions he or she cannot answer and go back to them at the end;
   - to re-read the text to find the answers.

Reading Test

Different views of Christmas

Contents

Information: **Christmas Celebrations**

From a novel: **'Christmas Eve', from** *Her Benny*

Poem: *They're Fetching in Ivy and Holly*

Christmas means different things to different people.

In these extracts, we look at different people's experiences and views of Christmas:

- from an information text about what Christmas means to Christians (a website to which people from different countries sent information)

- from a novel set about 125 years ago

- from a twentieth-century poem.

You have **15 minutes** to read through these passages.

Christmas Celebrations

People around the world celebrate Christmas in different ways, both religious and non-religious. Many celebrations are based on legends and traditions which pre-date Christianity, and important dates in the Christian calendar (such as Epiphany, on 6 January) are sometimes linked with the dates of pagan festivals. Many celebrations include the traditional foods of a country and many are influenced by the climate of the country.

Mexico

As Christmas approaches, elaborately decorated market stalls are set up in town centres to sell crafts, foods such as cheese, bananas, nuts and cookies, and flowers such as orchids and poinsettias.

There is a legend about the poinsettia. A little boy gathered some green branches from along the roadside while he was walking to church to look at the Nativity scene (the birth of Jesus). Other children laughed when he laid them by the manger as an offering, but they fell silent when a brilliant red, star-shaped flower appeared on each branch.

Processions which enact Joseph and Mary's search for somewhere to stay in Bethlehem on the night Jesus was born begin nine days before Christmas, because Mary and Joseph's journey from Nazareth to Bethlehem took nine days. People form two groups: pilgrims and innkeepers. The pilgrims trudge from house to house asking for shelter. The innkeepers turn them away until they reach the house in which an altar and Nativity scene have been set up. They go in with great rejoicing, a traditional prayer is spoken, and the party begins.

Sweden

The 'Yule log' comes from Scandinavia. Traditions concerned with warmth and light arose because of the long, dark, cold winters. Yuletide means 'the turning of the sun' (the winter solstice). It was traditionally a time when fortunes for the coming year were determined and when the dead were thought to walk the earth.

Originally an entire tree was brought into the house with great ceremony. The bottom of the trunk was set into the hearth so that the rest of the tree stuck out into the room. It was burned until 6 January (the end of Yule).

A thousand years ago in Sweden, the king declared that Christmas would last a month, from the feast of Saint Lucia (13 December) until Saint Knut's Day (13 January). Lucia, a 4th-century Sicilian saint and martyr, took food to Christians hiding from persecution in dark underground tunnels. To light the way she wore a wreath of candles on her head. She was discovered and killed. It is not known why she came to be revered in Sweden.

Schools, businesses and communities sponsor processions of girls wearing white dresses and wreaths of candles; carols are sung and the Queen of Light is thanked for bringing hope at the darkest time of the year.

On Christmas Eve a Christmas gnome emerges from his home under the floor of the house or the barn. He brings a sack of gifts.

Reading Test

Nicaragua
In Nicaragua, Christmas begins on 7 December with *La Griteria* (The Calling), when groups of people call at each house in the neighbourhood singing joyful hymns to the Virgin Mary. The singers are given sweets and other small gifts. A giant doll, *La Gigantona* (The Female Giant), a symbol of Mary, is paraded dancing through the streets to the accompaniment of drums.

Japan
Christmas became popular in Japan at the beginning of the 20th century because of the Christmas products made there for other countries. It is a non-religious holiday devoted to children, and is celebrated mainly in cities.

Tinsel and lights are hung in dance halls, cafes and pinball parlours. Trees are decorated with small toys, dolls, gold paper fans and lanterns, wind chimes, candles and paper ornaments including origami swans.

Japanese children call Santa 'Santa Kuroshu'. He is believed to have eyes in the back of his head – to watch the children all year long!

Jamaica
On Christmas morning, processions of *jonkonoo* (masked dancing men) parade down the streets, beating drums to herald Christmas Day.

Ghana
In Ghana, Christmas celebrations go on for eight days. Children are given new clothes and other gifts. Bells ring all morning to call people to church.

The main dish for Christmas day dinner is usually made from a fowl, goat or sheep. Yams and a soup made of meat and eggs are served.

In most towns, groups of children go from house to house, singing or chanting and blowing home-made trumpets throughout the eight days.

Iceland
Icelandic tradition has thirteen *Jolasveinar* (Christmas elves). Jolasveinar first appeared in the 17th century – the sons of the ogres Gryla and Leppaludi, who themselves had appeared in the 13th century and were said to have stolen and eaten naughty children.

They live in mountains and start to arrive in towns, one a day, thirteen days before Christmas Eve, with the last one arriving that morning. As their names suggest, the Jolasveinar are playful imps who steal the seasonal food and play tricks: Door Slammer awakens sleepers by slamming doors; Candle Beggar snatches candles; and Meat Hooker tries to run off with the roast.

They also leave presents for children (in shoes the children have left on the windowsill the night before). If any children have been naughty, they leave a potato or some other reminder to be good. They start departing for home on Christmas Day, with the last one departing on Twelfth Night (6 January).

Reading Test

1 In which four countries are there special Christmas processions?

_____

_____

[2]

2 Which of the processions are linked with the Nativity?

_____

_____

[4]

What tells you this?

_____

_____

_____

_____

3 Which country's Christmas celebrations have arisen because of the weather or climate there?

_____

_____

[1]

4 Give three examples of celebrations which are based on legends not connected with the Nativity.

_____

_____

_____

_____

[3]

TOTAL 10

Reading Test

5 What is the main similarity between Christmas celebrations in Sweden and Iceland?

_____
_____
_____
_____

6 Japan is not a Christian country. What made the Japanese begin to celebrate Christmas?

_____
_____
_____

7 In which two countries are children likely to make sure they behave themselves as Christmas approaches?

_____
_____

Explain your answer.

_____
_____
_____
_____

Reading Test

8 In which country does the Christmas season begin the earliest?

_____

9 In Sweden, what link is made between Saint Lucia and Yule?

_____
_____
_____

10 Which traditional festivals, in which countries, are linked with the date of the Christian festival of Epiphany?

_____
_____
_____
_____

Reading Test
Fiction

'Christmas Eve' from *Her Benny* by Silas Hocking

This book is set in Liverpool in the 1870s. Benny is ten and Nelly is nine years old. They make a living by selling matches. Benny also carries people's bags to and from the ferry-boats.

On Christmas Eve Benny took his sister through St John's Market, and highly delighted they were with what they saw. The thousands of geese, turkeys and pheasants, the loads of vegetables, the heaps of oranges and apples, the pyramids of every other conceivable kind of fruit, the stalls of sweetmeats, the tons of toffee, and the crowds of well-dressed people all bent upon buying something, were sources of infinite pleasure to the children. There was only one drawback to their happiness – they did not know how to lay out the sixpence they had brought with them to spend. If there had been less variety there would have been less difficulty; but, as it was, Benny felt as if he would never be able to decide what to buy. However, they agreed at last to lay out twopence for two slices of bread and ham, for they were both rather hungry; and then they spent the other fourpence on apples, oranges and toffee and, on the whole, felt very well satisfied with the result of their outlay.

It was rather later than usual when they got home, but old Betty knew where they had gone and, as it was Christmas Eve, she had got a bigger fire in than usual and had also got them a cup of hot cocoa each and some bunloaf to eat with it.

"By golly!" said Benny, as he munched the cake, "I do wish folks 'ud 'ave Christmas ev'ry week."

"You are a curious boy," said the old woman, looking up with a smile on her wrinkled face.

"Is I, Granny? I specks it's in my blood, as the chap said o' his timber leg."

The old woman had told them on the first evening of their arrival, when they had seemed at a loss what name to give her, to call her 'Granny'; and no name could have been more appropriate, or have come more readily to the children's lips.

"But could folks 'ave Christmas any oftener if they wished to?" asked little Nell.

"Of course they could, Nell," burst out Benny. "You dunna seem to know what folks make Christmas for."

"An' I thinks you dunno either, Benny."

"Don't I, though?" he said, putting on an air of importance. "It's made to give folks the chance of doing a lot o' feeding; didn't yer see all the gooses an' other nice things in the market that folks is going to polish off tomorrow?"

"I dunna think it was made purpose for that. Wur it now, Granny?"

Thus appealed to, the old woman, who had listened with an amused smile on her face, answered, "No, my child. It's called Christmas because it is the birthday of Christ."

"Who's he?" said Benny, looking up, while Nelly's eyes echoed the enquiry.

"Don't you know – ain't you never heerd?" said the old woman in a tone of surprise.

"Nay," said Benny, "nuthin' sense."

"Poor little dears! I didn't know as how you was so ignorant, or I should have told you before." And the old woman looked as if she did not know where or how to begin to tell the children the wonderful story, and for a considerable time remained silent. At length she said, "I'll read it to 'ee out o' the Book; mebbe you'll understand it better that way nor any way else."

And, taking down from a shelf her big and much-worn Bible, she opened it and began to read:

"Now when Jesus was born in Bethlehem of Judea …" And slowly the old woman read on until she reached the end of the chapter, while the children listened with wide and wondering eyes. To Nelly the words seemed like a revelation, responding to the deepest feeling in her nature, and awakening thoughts within her that were too big for utterance. Benny, however, could see nothing particularly interesting in the narrative itself. But the art of reading was to him a mystery past all comprehension. How Granny could see that story upon the pages of her Bible was altogether beyond his grasp. At length, after scratching his head vigorously for some time, he burst out:

"By jabbers! I's got it at last! Jimmy Jones squeeze me if I ain't! It's the specks that does it!"

"Does what?" said Nelly.

"Why, the story bizness, to be sure. Let me look at the book through your specks, shall I, Granny?"

"Ay, if you like, Benny." And the next minute he was looking at the Bible with Granny's spectacles astride his nose and an expression of disappointment upon his face.

"Golly! I's sold!" was his exclamation. "But this are a poser, and no mistake."

"What's such a poser?" said Granny.

"Why, how yer find the story in the book; for I can see nowt."

Reading Test

1 What made it difficult for the children to spend their sixpence?

| everything cost more than sixpence | they had to hurry because it was late | there was too much choice | they didn't see anything they wanted |

2 Who was old Betty?

| the children's grandmother | the person they lived with | their mother | their neighbour |

3 What impressed Benny most about Christmas?

| the food | it was Christ's birthday | the snow | the money people spent |

4 What surprised old Betty?

| the amount of food the children ate | they had money to spend | they were late coming home | they didn't know who Christ was |

5 Why was Betty silent for quite a long time?

| she didn't know how or where to begin telling them the story of Christ | she was speechless at their ignorance | the children were arguing about what Christmas was for | she was day-dreaming |

6 What does Benny mean by 'I specks'?

| a pair of glasses | the text on a page | I expect | my place |

Reading Test

7 Do you think the children go to school?
_____

How can you tell?
_____
_____

2

8 List three different exclamations of surprise used by Benny.
_____
_____
_____

3

9 What does Benny mean by 'Jimmy Jones squeeze me if I ain't'?
_____
_____
_____
_____

1

10 From the dialogue, give:

four examples in which verbs and pronouns do not agree
_____
_____

a non-standard plural _____
a non-standard past tense _____
a double negative _____

5

TOTAL

11

37

Reading Test

11 List four dialect words (other than exclamations) which the characters use, and their meanings.

_____
_____
_____
_____

2

12 What was the atmosphere of St John's Market like?

_____

2

How does the author create this atmosphere?

_____
_____
_____

13 Give three examples of alliteration in the description of the market.

_____
_____
_____

2

14 What was the main difference between the responses of Benny and Nell to the story?

_____
_____
_____
_____

2

TOTAL

8

Reading Test

15 How does the author help the reader to imagine the characters' accents?

_____
_____

Give four examples.

_____
_____

16 What can you tell about the narrator's religious beliefs?

_____

How can you tell?

_____
_____
_____
_____
_____

Reading Test
Poetry

They're Fetching in Ivy and Holly

"They're fetching in ivy and holly
And putting it this way and that.
I simply can't think of the reason,"
Said Si-Si the Siamese cat.

"They're pinning up lanterns and streamers.
There's mistletoe over the door.
They've brought in a tree from the garden.
I do wish I knew what it's for.

"It's covered with little glass candles
That go on and off without stop.
They've put it to stand in a corner
And tied up a fairy on top.

"They're stringing bright cards by the dozen
And letting them hang in a row.
Some people outside in the roadway
Are singing a song in the snow.

"I saw all the children write letters
And – I'm not at all sure this was wise –
They posted each one *up the chimney*.
I couldn't believe my own eyes.

"What on earth, in the middle of winter,
Does the family think it is at?
Won't somebody come and tell me?"
Said Si-Si the Siamese cat.

Charles Causley

Reading Test

1. How can you tell that this poem is about Christmas? Give three examples which tell you this.

2. Does Si-Si the cat think there must be a reason for the unusual goings-on?

   How can you tell?

3. What amazes the cat most of all?

4. Give three examples of lines which express the cat's puzzlement.

Reading Test

5 What does this poem have to do with the Christian view of Christmas? Explain your answer.

_____
_____
_____
_____
_____

6 What is the poet saying about the way in which people celebrate Christmas?

_____
_____
_____
_____
_____
_____
_____

2

3

TOTAL

5

English Test
Writing Test

This test helps you to gain an insight into your child's ability to write independently and to communicate meaning to the reader using the conventions of punctuation, spelling and handwriting.

The Writing Test covers the writing of:

- fiction
- information.

> Your child should first have read the passages in the Reading Tests.
>
> Allow 60 minutes for the Writing Test: a story *or* information writing.
>
> An indication of National Curriculum levels is given on pages 51–52.

1. Read the starting point aloud.
2. **FOR FICTION:** Introduce the planning sheet and discuss the headings on it. Emphasise the importance of:
   - writing a whole story and not just part of it
   - planning the story
   - thinking of a good opening to make the reader want to read on
   - keeping the reader interested
   - introducing the setting, the main character and the plot early in the story
   - helping the reader to get to know the characters
   - thinking of a good ending, rather than stopping abruptly.

   FOR INFORMATION: Discuss the points on the planning sheet. Emphasise the importance of:
   - thinking up a good introduction to make the reader want to read on
   - keeping the reader interested
   - making the text easy for the reader to follow
   - thinking of a good ending so that the information does not just 'tail off'.
3. Point out that grammar, spelling and punctuation are important.
4. If your child finishes before 60 minutes are up, encourage him or her to read through what he or she has written to look for anything which can be improved and to check grammar, spelling and punctuation.

Writing Test

> **Instructions**
>
> Choose **one** piece of writing from the two in this section.
> Plan and organise your ideas.
> You have 15 minutes in which to think about what to write and to make notes about your ideas.
> You have 45 minutes to do the writing.

Fiction
Making sense of Christmas

Read the extract from *Her Benny* and the poem *They're Fetching in Ivy and Holly*. Write a story from the point of view of a visitor from another planet who has observed people celebrating Christmas and is trying to make sense of what he or she observes.

Use the planning sheet on page 45.

Information
Christmas celebrations in the United Kingdom.

Write a report for a website about the ways in which people in the United Kingdom celebrate Christmas.

Use the planning sheet on page 46.

Writing Test
Planning Sheet: Fiction

Title

Setting

Where does the story take place?

When does it take place?

Characters

Name them and make notes about their personal qualities and characteristics.

Who is the main character or the narrator?

Who are the other characters?

Opening

Think of an opening which sets the scene and interests the reader.

Middle

Plan this section in paragraphs: what is each paragraph about?

Ending

How does the story end? Have you forgotten anything?

Writing Test
Planning Sheet: Information

On a flow-chart like this write everything you know about the ways in which people celebrate Christmas in the United Kingdom. Use arrows to begin to organise the pieces of information. This will help you to think of suitable sub-headings.

UK CHRISTMAS CELEBRATIONS

Decide in which person you should write, how formal or informal your writing should be, and whether it should be mainly active or passive.

Make notes of useful words or phrases.

Make notes of useful connective words.

Plan the contents of each paragraph.

Think of a suitable introduction and conclusion.

Spelling and Handwriting Test
Instructions

Spelling Test

The Spelling Test contains words which are generally known at the end of Key Stage 2; they include many of the spelling strategies, conventions and rules suggested for Year 6 in the National Literacy Strategy *Framework for Teaching*.

> This test is a short passage with words missed out.
> You read aloud from page 53 (the answers).
> Your child should write on page 48.
> Allow 10 minutes for the Spelling Test.
> At the end of the test, give a mark for each correct word and enter it in the space provided.
> National Curriculum levels are given on page 53.

1. Ask your child to listen to you reading the complete text.
2. Ask the child to look at his or her copy of the text. Point out that some of the words have been left out.
3. Tell your child that you are going to read the text again and that he or she should write in the missing words as you read. The missing words are in bold type on your copy of the text (page 53).
4. Read the text aloud again, pausing after each word in bold type, to give your child time to write it on the test copy.

You can repeat each of the bold words up to three times, if necessary.

Handwriting Test

1. Read the instructions with your child.
2. He or she should copy the passage onto the lines provided.
3. The National Curriculum guidelines on page 53 will help you to judge your child's level in handwriting.

Spelling Test

Where did Christmas cards _____ ?

This _____ way of _____ seasonal _____ began in the nineteenth _____.

An artist named W C T Dodgson is _____ to have made and sent the first Christmas card, in 1844. It led to the _____ of the first _____ Christmas card by Sir Henry Cole and J C Horsley in 1846. The card showed members of a _____ enjoying a glass of wine (a wassail cup): this was _____ by the Temperance Society, which was doing a great deal of work in cities like Manchester, Leeds and London to _____ people not to drink _____. By the 1870s, _____ cards were _____. They included _____ Christmas _____, symbols such as holly, _____, mistletoe, _____ and _____, as well as the Nativity: the stable, angels and _____.

TOTAL 20

48

Handwriting Test

Here is a short passage. Write it out very neatly in your usual handwriting. You will be given a mark for your handwriting. Make your writing as neat as possible, joining your letters.

Why do people decorate Christmas trees? The custom is linked with the Yule log of Scandinavian countries and it was introduced to Britain from Germany in 1840 by Queen Victoria's husband, Prince Albert of Saxe-Coburg. He also brought the tradition of Santa Claus riding on a sleigh pulled by reindeer.

LEVEL

Answers
Reading Test

Question number	Answer	Mark
INFORMATION: CHRISTMAS EVE		
1	Mexico, Sweden, Nicaragua and Jamaica.	2 (1 mark if two or three are named)
2	The processions in Nicaragua and Mexico. In Nicaragua, people sing hymns to the Virgin Mary. In Mexico, the processions enact Mary and Joseph's search for somewhere to stay.	2 2
3	Sweden.	1
4	The Yule log, St Lucia's Day in Sweden and the *Jolasveinar* in Iceland.	3
5	Gnomes or elves bring gifts *or* they end on 6 January.	1
6	They made Christmas products for other countries.	1
7	Iceland and Japan. In Iceland, the elves only leave presents for children who have been good; if they have been naughty the elves leave a potato or some other reminder to behave themselves. In Japan, Santa watches what they are doing all through the year.	1 2
8	Nicaragua.	1
9	Yule festivals are about light and warmth. Saint Lucia had a wreath of candles to light her way along dark passages.	3 marks for a complete answer. 1 mark if light is mentioned.
10	In Iceland, the *Jolasveinar* leave on 6 January, and in Sweden the Yule log is burned until 6 January.	2
FICTION: HER BENNY		
1	There was too much choice.	1
2	The person they lived with.	1
3	The food.	1
4	They didn't know who Christ was.	1
5	She didn't know how or where to begin telling them the story of Christ.	1
6	I expect.	1
7	No. They cannot read *or* they have never heard the story of the Nativity.	1 1
8	By golly! By jabbers! Golly! I's sold!	1 mark for each. Maximum 3.
9	He is stressing that *he knows* how Betty can read the story from the page *or* It is the same as saying 'I'll eat my hat …'	1
10	Is I?, I thinks, folks is, Wur it, chaps says, I says, you was, I's got it, it's the specks that does it, I's sold!, I never knowed, this are. Gooses. I never knowed Ain't you never heerd?	2 marks for four. 1 mark for one to three 1 1 1
11	I specks (I expect), specks (glasses/spectacles), dunna (do not/don't), 'polish off' (eat), 'ee (you), ain't (are not/ have not), dunno (don't know), nowt (nothing)	2 marks for four, 1 mark for one to three.
12	Busy and full of Christmas foods. 'Crowds of people' and lists of the things the children see, with words which give the impression of large amounts, like thousands, heaps, tons and loads.	1 1
13	stalls of sweetmeats, tons of toffee, bent upon buying.	2 marks for all three. 1 mark for one or two.
14	Benny was impressed by the way Betty could read a story from the marks on the pages, but Nelly was fascinated by the story itself.	2
15	He does not use normal spelling, but spells the words in the way in which people said them: ud 'ave (would have), o' (of), dunna (don't), dunno (don't know), an' (and), yer (you), wur (were), heerd (heard), nuthin (nothing), mebbe (maybe), bizness (business).	2 1 mark if four examples are given.
16	He is a Christian. He calls the story of Christ 'the wonderful story'. The story suggests that the children ought to know about it.	3 2 marks for both observations; 1 mark for one of them.
POETRY: THEY'RE FETCHING IN IVY AND HOLLY		
1	It mentions: holly and ivy; people pinning up lanterns and streamers; mistletoe; a tree covered with glass candles and with a fairy on top; cards; children posting letters up the chimney to Santa Claus.	1 mark each. Maximum 3.
2	Yes. It can't think of the reason. It asks someone to tell it.	1 2
3	That children posted letters up the chimney.	1
4	I simply can't think of a reason … I do wish I knew what it's for, I couldn't believe my own eyes … Won't somebody come and tell me?	1 mark each Maximum 3.
5	Nothing. There is no mention of the Nativity or Christ.	2
6	Their actions have nothing to do with Christmas or At Christmas people go mad/ lose their senses/ do silly things. or Christmas has no real meaning for some people.	3

Answers
Writing Test

There are three aspects to consider in your child's achievement in writing:

1. Organisation and purpose (the content of the story or, in information writing, the form and content of the text).

2. Grammar (the correct use of punctuation, capital letters, tenses and pronouns).

3. Style (use of connective words, sentence structure and vocabulary).

Your child might do better in one of these aspects than in the others. Looking at his or her writing in this way helps to pinpoint strengths and weaknesses.

The following simplified descriptions will help you to gain an idea of your child's level in writing.

ORGANISATION AND PURPOSE

Fiction writing

Level 3	Level 4	Level 5
• The child has thought about the structure of the story and does not just list one event after another. • Some description is given of the setting and characters. • The child has thought about the atmosphere of the story: excitement, calm, sadness.	• The child has separated the beginning, middle (or the events which take place) and the ending into paragraphs. • The events are linked in a logical way. • The characters respond to each other's words and actions. The characters develop as the story progresses.	• There is a good structure and the child shows a good grasp of the narrative form. Dialogue is mixed with events and description. • The reader's interest is kept through the use of techniques such as dialogue and change of place and time. The child makes comments on what is happening and indicates the thoughts or feelings of characters. • The opening, main events and ending are divided by paragraphs.

Information writing

Level 3	Level 4	Level 5
• As well as a title, sub-headings are used. • There is a sentence of introduction. • Some connection is made between points. • There is some attempt at explanation.	• There is a title. • Sub-headings are carefully sequenced. Some paragraphs are used within the sections. • There is an introduction. • Points are sequenced with care. • There is a conclusion (the writing does not just end). • All the information a reader needs is included.	• The child uses conventions of layout (eg sub-headings, bullet-points) competently. • The text is tailored to the reader (for example, by an introduction to engage interest and set out the purpose of the text). • Points are linked and set out in a logical order, and there is a suitable conclusion. • The argument is well structured and convincing.

Writing Test Answers

GRAMMAR

Level 3	Level 4	Level 5
• At least half of the sentences on the first page start with a capital letter and finish with a full stop, exclamation mark or question mark.	• At least three quarters of the sentences on the first page start with a capital letter and finish with a full stop, question mark or exclamation mark. • Commas are used to separate parts of a sentence or items in a list. • The tense is consistent. • Quotation marks are used to show where direct speech begins and ends in at least half of the instances. • Pronouns are consistent (for example, there is no sudden change from 'he' or 'she' to 'I').	• There are few sentences without the correct use of capital letters and full stops, exclamation marks or question marks. Capital letters are used to begin proper nouns. • Commas and speech marks are used appropriately. • Other punctuation is used: for example, dashes and brackets.

STYLE

Fiction Writing

Level 3	Level 4	Level 5
• The sentence structures are more like those of written than spoken language. • Connectives are used to show contrast, to connect time and for explanation: 'but', 'when', 'also', 'so', 'because'.	• The style is different from spoken language: it has the form of written language. • More complex connectives are used: 'when', 'although', 'if', 'in the meantime'. • Interesting words and phrases make the writing more effective: 'she wrapped some roller skates in red paper and tied a gold bow around it', 'a plain, ordinary piece of twig seemed to make everyone giggle'.	• Both simple and complex sentences are used appropriately. Imaginative vocabulary is used. The child conveys meaning through precise use of language. • He or she makes appropriate choices about the use of standard or non-standard English, including dialogue words and colloquial expressions.

Information Writing

Level 3	Level 4	Level 5
• The sentence structures are more like those of written than spoken language. • Connectives are used to show contrast, to connect time and for explanation: 'but', 'when', 'also', 'so', 'because'. • Vocabulary includes words such as 'slightly', 'respect'.	• The style is different from spoken language; it has the form of written language. • More complex connectives are used: 'when', 'although', 'if', 'in the meantime'. • Interesting words and phrases make the writing more effective.	• More than one type of sentence structure and length is used to add interest. • The child can use both active and passive verbs (for example 'People gave one another presents'/'presents were given'). • Repetition is avoided by words such as 'it', 'they', 'which'. • The child can judge whether or not the tone of the writing should be formal or informal.

Answers
Spelling Test

Where did Christmas cards **originate**? This **popular** way of **exchanging** seasonal **greetings** began in the nineteenth **century**. An artist named W C T Dodgson is **thought** to have made and sent the first Christmas card, in 1844. It led to the **production** of the first **commercial** Christmas card by Sir Henry Cole and J C Horsley in 1846. The card showed members of a **family** enjoying a glass of wine (a wassail cup): this was **condemned** by the Temperance Society, which was doing a great deal of work in cities like Manchester, Leeds and London to **persuade** people not to drink **alcohol**. By the 1870s, **manufactured** cards were **commonplace**. They included **traditional** Christmas **scenes**, symbols such as holly, **ivy**, mistletoe, **lanterns** and **candles**, as well as the Nativity: the stable, angels and **shepherds**.

National Curriculum Levels
English

Use the conversion tables below to gain an idea of your child's National Curriculum level in Reading, Spelling and Handwriting. For Writing, refer back to the National Curriculum level charts on pages 51 to 52.

Information Reading	
Mark	Level
0 – 3	Below Level 2
4 – 7	Level 2
8 – 12	Level 3
13 – 18	Level 4
19 – 21	Level 5

Fiction Reading	
Mark	Level
0 – 5	Below Level 2
6 – 12	Level 2
13 – 21	Level 3
22 – 26	Level 4
27 – 30	Level 5

Poetry Reading	
0 – 2	Below Level 2
3 – 6	Level 2
7 – 10	Level 3
11 – 13	Level 4
14 – 15	Level 5

Spelling	
0 – 3	Below Level 2
4 – 8	Level 2
9 – 13	Level 3
14 – 17	Level 4
18 – 20	Level 5

Handwriting	
Indications	**Level**
Only some letters recognisable	Below Level 2
Most letters formed correctly, with no random mixing of upper and lower cases	Level 2
Clear and legible	Level 3
Legible and more fluent. Letters are joined and their size is regular. Words are evenly spaced.	Level 4
A clear, legible, joined style.	Level 5

If your child needs more practice in any English topics, use the WHSmith Key Stage 2 English Revision Guide.

Science

Science at Key Stage 2

Most children at Key Stage 2 attain levels 3 to 4 in Science, but some may attain level 5 or even level 6.

This performance at the different levels is summarised below.

Level 3	Level 4	Level 5	Level 6
Children can describe differences and provide simple explanations. They can sort materials and living things and offer ideas about why materials are suitable for their purpose. When explaining how things work they link cause and effect, such as suggesting that the lack of light causes plants to become yellow. They also make generalisations about things they see, such as suggesting that it is difficult to see dim lights if they are near very bright lights.	Children can use more scientific terms such as the names of the organs of the body and those of flowering plants. They can use technical terms to describe processes such as evaporation and condensation. They can explain how differences are used to classify materials and living things systematically. They use their ideas about the way the physical world works when explaining how shadows are formed or the way that sound is heard through different materials.	Children can explain the factors behind why different organisms are found in different environments. They can describe the properties of metals and how they are distinct from other materials. They can identify why changes occur in materials and can suggest ways in which specific mixtures can be separated. They can use abstract ideas and models to explain physical phenomena such as the orbiting model of the earth to explain day and year length.	Children are familiar with cell structure and the cause of variation between living things. They will recognise that materials are made up from particles and be able to recognise how new materials are formed in chemical reactions. They should be able to explain phenomena which involve a number of factors.

Setting the test

Give your child plenty of time to do the test – 45 minutes should be about right.

The test can be a chance to confirm how well your child has done and how much he or she has learnt. Don't focus exclusively on what the child does not know.

Enter the mark in the box next to each question. Add the marks together at the end of each test. Look at page 63 for an indication of the level at which your child is working.

Science Test

Shadows

1 The children put a stick in the ground.
They record the length of its shadow at different times of the day.
They put their results on a graph.

[Bar chart: length of shadow (cm) vs time
- 8: 25
- 9: 18
- 10: 14
- 11: 10
- 12: 5]

a What makes the length of the shadow alter during the day?

_____

_____

1

b How else does the shadow change?

Tick one answer.

It gets thicker. ☐

It moves round the stick. ☐

It gets darker. ☐

1

TOTAL

2

55

Science Test

Bikes

2 Kerrie is checking her bike.
She checks to make sure that the brakes are rubbing on the wheels to make them stop quickly.

a What is the force which slows her down?
_____

1

b The wheels are stiff so she oils the axle.
How does this help?
_____

1

c Kerrie is not pedalling down the hill.
She is moving fast.
Draw the force of air resistance acting on this bike.

1

The water cycle

3 Add the correct word to each sentence to explain the water cycle.

evaporates   vapour   rain   condenses   flow

Water falls as _____ and runs into rivers.

Rivers _____ to the sea.

Water _____ into the air.

Water _____ is an invisible gas in the air.

Water _____ to a cloud.

4

TOTAL

7

56

Science Test

Mixtures

4 Some cereals are mixtures of bran, oats and dried fruit. Bill and Ben separated two cereals.

a Circle **two** things they could use for this.

They put bran, oats and dried fruit from each cereal in different piles and weighed them.
They recorded their results on pie charts:

Cereal A: 100 g   Cereal B: 100 g

b

	Cereal A	Cereal B
What fraction of the cereal was bran ?		
What weight of the cereal was bran ?		

c Fruit tastes sweet.

Which cereal would taste sweetest?

_____

d They mixed milk with each cereal. After an hour the milk had disappeared and the cereal had expanded.

What had happened?

_____

1

2

1

1

TOTAL

5

57

Science Test

Materials

5 a Sunil is making toffee. He has a wooden spoon or a metal spoon to stir the hot mixture. Which one should he use?
_____

b Explain your answer.
_____
_____

c Masie needs to take some cakes out of the oven. She has rubber gloves or fabric gloves to wear.
Which should she use?
_____

d Explain your answer.
_____
_____

6 Hamish and Lara are making sandcastles. Hamish has a full bucket of wet sand. Lara has a full bucket of dry sand. Both buckets are the same size.
Explain why Hamish's bucket feels heavier than Lara's.
_____
_____

7 Link the correct label to each part of this food chain. Use each word only once.

| prey | producer | predator | consumer |

lettuce   snail   thrush   cat

TOTAL: 9

Science Test

Fish tank

8 Tim measured the temperature of the water in his fish tank. He used a sensor attached to a computer to record the changes.
This is Tim's temperature chart.

a How long was the sensor in the tank?
_____

1

b What was the temperature of the water in the tank at first?
_____

1

c What was the temperature of the water at 9 pm?
_____

1

d Tim added some warm water to the tank. At what time did he do this?
_____

1

e Fish tanks are made from glass or plastic. Give two reasons why these materials are used.
_____
_____

1

TOTAL

5

Science Test

Plants

9 a Write a question which will help Sam to put these leaves into two different groups.

_____

_____

b John has listed the stages in the life cycle of a plant.

They are in the wrong order.

Number the sentences to show which order they should be in. (The first has been done for you.)

The flowers are pollinated. ☐

The seeds are dispersed. [1]

A root grows down. ☐

The plant grows and produces flowers. ☐

New seeds develop. ☐

TOTAL 5

Science Test

Health

10 Fred does not feel well.

   a What could he do to lead a more healthy life?

   _____

   _____

   1

   b Fred visits the dentist. She looks at his mouth.

   How many molars, incisors and fillings does he have?

molars	
incisors	
fillings (in molars)	

   3

   Tick **two** things he could do to reduce his chance of getting tooth decay.

   Buy toothpaste ☐

   Clean teeth after meals ☐

   Eat less sugary food ☐

   Wash his face more often ☐

   2

   TOTAL

   6

61

Science Test

Tadpoles

11 Jill and Ben made a graph to show the tadpoles and frogs they saw in the pond.

a How many tadpoles were there in May?
_____

b Why were there no tadpoles in August?
_____

c Suggest two reasons why there were only 3 frogs in August.
_____
_____

d Class 5 wrote about the way that tadpoles turn into frogs.

Put these stages into the correct order.

Frogs mate. ☐

Tadpole tail disappears to leave small froglet. ☐

Tadpoles grow legs. ☐

Female frog lays eggs called frog spawn. ☐

Tadpoles emerge from spawn. ☐

TOTAL 8

62